EMMANUEL JOSEPH

Words in Motion, The Intersection of Public Speaking, Leadership, and Bold Action

Copyright © 2025 by Emmanuel Joseph

All rights reserved. No part of this publication may be reproduced, stored or transmitted in any form or by any means, electronic, mechanical, photocopying, recording, scanning, or otherwise without written permission from the publisher. It is illegal to copy this book, post it to a website, or distribute it by any other means without permission.

First edition

This book was professionally typeset on Reedsy.
Find out more at reedsy.com

Contents

1	Chapter 1: The Power of Words	1
2	Chapter 2: The Evolution of Public Speaking	3
3	Chapter 3: Leadership Through Communication	4
4	Chapter 4: The Art of Persuasion	5
5	Chapter 5: The Role of Body Language	6
6	Chapter 6: Overcoming Fear and Building Confidence	7
7	Chapter 7: Crafting Compelling Stories	8
8	Chapter 8: The Impact of Emotional Intelligence	9
9	Chapter 9: Strategies for Effective Listening	10
10	Chapter 10: Navigating Difficult Conversations	11
11	Chapter 6: Overcoming Fear and Building Confidence	12
12	Chapter 7: Crafting Compelling Stories	14
13	Chapter 8: The Impact of Emotional Intelligence	16
14	Chapter 9: Strategies for Effective Listening	18
15	Chapter 10: Navigating Difficult Conversations	20
16	Chapter 11: Inspiring Bold Actions	22
17	Chapter 12: Balancing Authenticity and Professionalism	24
18	Chapter 13: The Ethics of Public Speaking and Leadership	26
19	Chapter 14: Utilizing Technology in Communication	28
20	Chapter 15: Building a Personal Brand	30
21	Chapter 16: The Future of Public Speaking and Leadership	32
22	Chapter 17: Putting It All Together: Actionable Steps	34

1

Chapter 1: The Power of Words

Words hold an extraordinary power that can inspire, persuade, and ignite change. Throughout history, great leaders have harnessed this power to unite people, create movements, and shape the future. In this chapter, we explore the profound influence of words and how they can be used effectively in public speaking and leadership.

Words can evoke emotions, paint vivid pictures, and convey complex ideas. A well-chosen word can lift someone's spirits, while a poorly chosen one can cause harm. The ability to articulate thoughts clearly and compellingly is a crucial skill for any leader. Through examples of influential speeches and moments in history, we delve into how words have shaped our world and continue to do so.

Public speaking is not just about delivering information; it is about connecting with an audience. The way words are delivered can be just as important as the words themselves. Tone, pace, and emphasis can all affect how a message is received. In this chapter, we discuss techniques for mastering these aspects of delivery to ensure that the power of words is fully realized.

Finally, we explore the responsibility that comes with the power of words. Leaders and public speakers must be mindful of their words' impact on their audience. With great power comes great responsibility, and understanding the ethical considerations of communication is essential for any aspiring leader.

2

Chapter 2: The Evolution of Public Speaking

Public speaking has evolved from the ancient forums of Greece and Rome to the modern-day podiums, virtual platforms, and social media channels. This chapter explores the historical journey of public speaking, highlighting key figures and moments that have shaped the art of oration. From Cicero and Demosthenes to Martin Luther King Jr. and Malala Yousafzai, we trace the lineage of influential speakers and the impact they have had on society.

We also examine the technological advancements that have transformed public speaking. The advent of radio, television, and the internet has expanded the reach of speakers and democratized the access to information. This chapter delves into how these changes have influenced the way leaders communicate and the strategies they employ to engage diverse audiences.

Finally, we consider the future of public speaking. With the rise of artificial intelligence, virtual reality, and other emerging technologies, the landscape of communication is continually shifting. We discuss the potential implications of these developments and how aspiring leaders can stay ahead of the curve.

Chapter 3: Leadership Through Communication

Effective leadership is rooted in the ability to communicate vision, inspire action, and build trust. In this chapter, we explore the symbiotic relationship between leadership and communication. We begin by defining the core attributes of a successful leader and how they manifest through verbal and non-verbal communication.

We then delve into the various styles of leadership communication, from authoritative and democratic to transformational and servant leadership. Each style has its own set of strengths and challenges, and understanding these nuances can help leaders tailor their approach to different situations and audiences.

Case studies of renowned leaders such as Nelson Mandela, Angela Merkel, and Steve Jobs illustrate the principles discussed in this chapter. Through these examples, we highlight the diverse ways in which leaders have harnessed the power of communication to achieve their goals and inspire others.

4

Chapter 4: The Art of Persuasion

Persuasion is a fundamental skill for any public speaker and leader. This chapter explores the psychology of persuasion and the techniques that can be used to influence others. We begin by examining the classical principles of rhetoric—ethos, pathos, and logos—and how they can be effectively employed in speeches and presentations.

We then discuss the importance of understanding the audience's needs, values, and motivations. By tailoring messages to resonate with the audience, speakers can create a stronger connection and increase their persuasive power. This chapter provides practical tips for conducting audience analysis and crafting messages that align with their interests.

Finally, we explore the ethical considerations of persuasion. While the goal is to influence, it is crucial to do so with integrity and respect for the audience. We discuss the boundaries of ethical persuasion and how leaders can maintain their credibility and trustworthiness.

5

Chapter 5: The Role of Body Language

Words alone are not enough to convey a message effectively; body language plays a crucial role in communication. This chapter delves into the significance of non-verbal cues and how they can enhance or undermine a speaker's message. We begin by exploring the basic elements of body language, including gestures, posture, eye contact, and facial expressions.

We then discuss how to develop self-awareness and control over one's body language. By practicing mindfulness and receiving feedback, speakers can become more conscious of their non-verbal signals and improve their overall communication skills. This chapter provides exercises and techniques for mastering body language and making a positive impression on the audience.

Finally, we consider the cultural variations in body language. Different cultures have different norms and interpretations of non-verbal cues, and it is essential for speakers to be aware of these differences to avoid misunderstandings and build rapport with diverse audiences.

6

Chapter 6: Overcoming Fear and Building Confidence

Public speaking can be a daunting task, even for seasoned leaders. This chapter focuses on strategies to overcome the fear of speaking in front of an audience and build confidence. We begin by understanding the root causes of public speaking anxiety and how it manifests physically and mentally.

We then explore practical techniques to manage and reduce anxiety, such as deep breathing exercises, visualization, and positive affirmations. By incorporating these practices into their routine, speakers can gradually build confidence and become more comfortable in front of an audience.

Additionally, we discuss the importance of preparation and practice. The more familiar a speaker is with their material and the more they rehearse, the more confident they will feel. This chapter provides tips for effective preparation, including creating outlines, practicing in front of a mirror, and seeking feedback from trusted peers.

7

Chapter 7: Crafting Compelling Stories

Stories have the power to captivate and resonate with audiences. This chapter delves into the art of storytelling and how it can be used to enhance public speaking and leadership. We begin by exploring the key elements of a compelling story, such as a relatable protagonist, a clear conflict, and a satisfying resolution.

We then discuss different types of stories that can be used in speeches, including personal anecdotes, historical events, and hypothetical scenarios. Each type of story serves a unique purpose and can be tailored to fit the speaker's message and audience.

The chapter also provides tips for crafting and delivering stories effectively. From setting the scene and building suspense to using vivid language and expressive gestures, we explore various techniques to bring stories to life and make a lasting impact on the audience.

8

Chapter 8: The Impact of Emotional Intelligence

Emotional intelligence (EI) is a crucial skill for effective communication and leadership. This chapter explores the role of EI in public speaking and how it can be developed and applied. We begin by defining the core components of EI, including self-awareness, self-regulation, motivation, empathy, and social skills.

We then discuss how these components influence communication and leadership. For example, self-awareness helps speakers recognize their own emotions and manage them effectively, while empathy allows them to connect with their audience on a deeper level.

This chapter also provides practical exercises to enhance EI, such as mindfulness meditation, journaling, and active listening. By cultivating EI, leaders can become more attuned to their own emotions and those of others, leading to more effective and impactful communication.

9

Chapter 9: Strategies for Effective Listening

Listening is an often-overlooked aspect of communication, yet it is essential for building trust and understanding. This chapter explores the importance of effective listening in leadership and public speaking. We begin by defining active listening and its key components, such as paying attention, reflecting, and responding.

We then discuss the barriers to effective listening, including distractions, biases, and preconceived notions. By identifying and addressing these barriers, leaders can improve their listening skills and foster more meaningful connections with their audience.

The chapter also provides practical strategies for becoming a better listener, such as maintaining eye contact, asking open-ended questions, and providing feedback. By mastering these techniques, leaders can demonstrate empathy, build rapport, and enhance their overall communication effectiveness.

10

Chapter 10: Navigating Difficult Conversations

Difficult conversations are an inevitable part of leadership. This chapter focuses on strategies for navigating challenging interactions with grace and effectiveness. We begin by identifying common types of difficult conversations, such as delivering bad news, addressing conflicts, and providing constructive feedback.

We then discuss the importance of preparation and setting the right tone for these conversations. By approaching difficult discussions with empathy, clarity, and respect, leaders can create a supportive environment that encourages open dialogue.

The chapter also provides practical tips for managing emotions, both for the speaker and the listener. Techniques such as staying calm, acknowledging feelings, and finding common ground can help diffuse tension and facilitate productive conversations.

11

Chapter 6: Overcoming Fear and Building Confidence

Public speaking can be a daunting task, even for seasoned leaders. This chapter focuses on strategies to overcome the fear of speaking in front of an audience and build confidence. The first step is to understand the root causes of public speaking anxiety, which often stem from fear of judgment, self-doubt, and past negative experiences. By acknowledging these fears and recognizing that they are common, speakers can begin to address them constructively.

Practical techniques to manage and reduce anxiety include deep breathing exercises, visualization, and positive affirmations. Deep breathing helps to calm the nervous system and reduce physical symptoms of anxiety, such as a racing heart and sweaty palms. Visualization involves imagining a successful speaking experience, which can help create a positive mindset. Positive affirmations, such as "I am confident and capable," can boost self-esteem and counteract negative thoughts.

Preparation and practice are also crucial for building confidence. The more familiar a speaker is with their material, the more comfortable they will feel. Creating detailed outlines, practicing in front of a mirror, and seeking feedback from trusted peers can help speakers refine their delivery and gain confidence. Additionally, practicing in front of smaller, supportive audiences can help ease the transition to larger, more intimidating groups.

Finally, adopting a growth mindset can make a significant difference. Embracing mistakes as opportunities for learning and improvement can reduce the pressure to be perfect. By focusing on progress rather than perfection, speakers can build resilience and confidence over time. Remember, even the most accomplished speakers started somewhere, and every experience is a step towards becoming more confident and effective.

12

Chapter 7: Crafting Compelling Stories

Stories have the power to captivate and resonate with audiences. This chapter delves into the art of storytelling and how it can be used to enhance public speaking and leadership. A compelling story includes a relatable protagonist, a clear conflict, and a satisfying resolution. These elements create a narrative arc that engages the audience and makes the message memorable.

Different types of stories serve unique purposes in speeches. Personal anecdotes can establish a connection with the audience, as they reveal the speaker's authenticity and vulnerability. Historical events can provide context and illustrate broader themes, while hypothetical scenarios can encourage the audience to envision possibilities and consider new perspectives. By incorporating a mix of these story types, speakers can create a rich and varied narrative.

Crafting and delivering stories effectively involves several techniques. Setting the scene with vivid descriptions helps the audience visualize the story. Building suspense by gradually revealing information keeps the audience engaged. Using expressive language and gestures brings the story to life and makes it more impactful. Practicing these techniques can help speakers develop their storytelling skills and make their messages more compelling.

Additionally, understanding the audience's needs and interests is crucial for crafting relevant stories. Tailoring stories to resonate with the audience's values and experiences can create a stronger connection and increase the overall effectiveness of the speech. By putting themselves in the audience's shoes, speakers can choose stories that are not only entertaining but also meaningful and impactful.

Chapter 8: The Impact of Emotional Intelligence

Emotional intelligence (EI) is a crucial skill for effective communication and leadership. This chapter explores the role of EI in public speaking and how it can be developed and applied. The core components of EI include self-awareness, self-regulation, motivation, empathy, and social skills. These elements influence how individuals perceive, understand, and manage emotions, both their own and those of others.

Self-awareness involves recognizing one's emotions and how they affect thoughts and behavior. By understanding their emotional triggers, speakers can manage their reactions and maintain composure during challenging situations. Self-regulation refers to the ability to control impulsive responses and adapt to changing circumstances. This skill allows speakers to remain calm and focused, even under pressure.

Empathy, the ability to understand and share the feelings of others, is essential for connecting with an audience. By tuning into the audience's emotions and perspectives, speakers can tailor their messages to resonate more deeply. Social skills, including active listening and effective communication, enhance interactions and build rapport. Developing these skills can help speakers navigate complex social dynamics and foster positive relationships.

Practical exercises to enhance EI include mindfulness meditation, journaling, and active listening. Mindfulness meditation helps individuals become more aware of their emotions and reactions. Journaling provides a reflective space to explore thoughts and feelings. Active listening involves fully engaging with others, paying attention to verbal and non-verbal cues, and responding thoughtfully. By cultivating EI, leaders can improve their communication, build stronger connections, and lead more effectively.

Chapter 9: Strategies for Effective Listening

Listening is an often-overlooked aspect of communication, yet it is essential for building trust and understanding. This chapter explores the importance of effective listening in leadership and public speaking. Active listening involves fully engaging with the speaker, paying attention, reflecting, and responding. It demonstrates empathy and respect, fostering a positive and collaborative environment.

Barriers to effective listening include distractions, biases, and preconceived notions. Distractions, such as electronic devices or environmental noise, can prevent individuals from fully focusing on the speaker. Biases and preconceived notions can distort the interpretation of the message and hinder open-mindedness. Recognizing and addressing these barriers is crucial for improving listening skills and fostering genuine understanding.

Practical strategies for becoming a better listener include maintaining eye contact, asking open-ended questions, and providing feedback. Maintaining eye contact shows the speaker that they have the listener's full attention. Open-ended questions encourage the speaker to elaborate and provide more information, leading to a deeper understanding. Providing feedback, such as summarizing key points or expressing empathy, validates the speaker's message and strengthens the connection.

CHAPTER 9: STRATEGIES FOR EFFECTIVE LISTENING

Effective listening also involves being present in the moment and withholding judgment. Being present means focusing on the speaker and the conversation, rather than thinking about what to say next or being distracted by other thoughts. Withholding judgment allows the listener to fully understand the speaker's perspective without immediately forming opinions or conclusions. By mastering these techniques, leaders can demonstrate empathy, build rapport, and enhance their overall communication effectiveness.

15

Chapter 10: Navigating Difficult Conversations

Difficult conversations are an inevitable part of leadership. This chapter focuses on strategies for navigating challenging interactions with grace and effectiveness. To begin, it's essential to identify common types of difficult conversations, such as delivering bad news, addressing conflicts, and providing constructive feedback. Understanding the context and purpose of these conversations helps in preparing for them effectively.

Preparation is key to handling difficult conversations. Setting the right tone is crucial, and this involves approaching discussions with empathy, clarity, and respect. Empathy allows leaders to understand and acknowledge the feelings of others, while clarity ensures that the message is conveyed without ambiguity. Respect creates a supportive environment that encourages open dialogue and reduces defensiveness.

Managing emotions during difficult conversations is another critical aspect. Techniques such as staying calm, acknowledging feelings, and finding common ground can help diffuse tension and facilitate productive discussions. It's important to remain composed and focused on the issue at hand, rather than getting sidetracked by emotional reactions. By doing so, leaders can guide conversations towards constructive outcomes.

CHAPTER 10: NAVIGATING DIFFICULT CONVERSATIONS

Finally, it's essential to follow up on difficult conversations. Ensuring that any agreements or action points are implemented demonstrates commitment and accountability. It also provides an opportunity to check in with the individuals involved, address any lingering concerns, and reinforce positive behaviors. Effective follow-up helps build trust and reinforces the leader's credibility.

Chapter 11: Inspiring Bold Actions

Leadership is not just about managing people and processes; it's about inspiring bold actions that drive change and innovation. This chapter explores the ways in which leaders can motivate their teams to take courageous steps and pursue ambitious goals. The foundation of inspiring bold actions lies in a clear and compelling vision that aligns with the values and aspirations of the team.

Communicating this vision effectively is crucial. Leaders must use powerful language and vivid imagery to paint a picture of the future they envision. By sharing stories of past successes and overcoming challenges, they can create a sense of possibility and excitement. It's also important to articulate the purpose and impact of the bold actions, highlighting how they contribute to the greater good.

Empowerment plays a significant role in inspiring bold actions. Leaders must create an environment where team members feel trusted and supported to take risks and innovate. Providing autonomy, resources, and encouragement fosters a sense of ownership and accountability. Recognizing and celebrating bold actions, regardless of the outcome, reinforces a culture of courage and continuous improvement.

Lastly, leading by example is essential. Leaders who demonstrate boldness in their actions and decisions inspire others to follow suit. Whether it's tackling a difficult project, addressing a sensitive issue, or championing a new initiative, leaders set the tone for what is possible. By embodying the values and behaviors they wish to see in others, leaders can cultivate a culture of boldness and innovation.

Chapter 12: Balancing Authenticity and Professionalism

Authenticity and professionalism are both critical components of effective leadership and public speaking. This chapter delves into the delicate balance between being true to oneself and maintaining a professional demeanor. Authenticity involves being genuine, transparent, and consistent in one's actions and communication. It builds trust and fosters meaningful connections with others.

However, authenticity must be balanced with professionalism, which encompasses respect, competence, and adherence to ethical standards. Professionalism ensures that leaders are taken seriously and that their actions and decisions are credible. It's important to recognize that authenticity does not mean sharing every thought or feeling; rather, it's about being sincere and true to one's values while considering the context and audience.

Navigating this balance requires self-awareness and emotional intelligence. Leaders must understand their strengths, weaknesses, and triggers, and how these impact their interactions with others. They should also be attuned to the needs and expectations of their audience, adapting their communication style accordingly. This chapter provides practical tips for achieving this balance, such as setting boundaries, practicing active listening, and seeking feedback.

Finally, we explore the challenges and benefits of balancing authenticity and professionalism. While it can be challenging to navigate complex social dynamics and varying expectations, the rewards are significant. Leaders who strike this balance can build strong, trusting relationships, foster a positive and inclusive culture, and enhance their overall effectiveness and impact.

18

Chapter 13: The Ethics of Public Speaking and Leadership

Ethics play a fundamental role in public speaking and leadership. This chapter examines the ethical considerations that leaders and speakers must navigate to maintain their integrity and credibility. Ethical communication involves honesty, transparency, and respect for the audience. Leaders must ensure that their messages are truthful, accurate, and free from manipulation or deception.

One of the key ethical challenges in public speaking is balancing persuasion with respect for the audience's autonomy. While the goal is to influence, it is crucial to do so with integrity and respect for the audience's right to make informed decisions. This involves avoiding coercive tactics, exaggerations, and false claims. Leaders must also be mindful of the power dynamics at play and strive to create an inclusive and respectful environment.

Ethical leadership extends beyond communication to encompass actions and decisions. Leaders must model ethical behavior and hold themselves and others accountable. This includes making decisions that align with their values and the greater good, even when faced with difficult choices. It also involves creating a culture of integrity, where ethical behavior is recognized and rewarded.

Finally, we discuss the importance of continuous reflection and learning in ethical leadership. Ethical dilemmas are often complex and context-specific, requiring leaders to navigate gray areas and make nuanced judgments. By engaging in ongoing reflection, seeking diverse perspectives, and staying informed about ethical standards and best practices, leaders can continually enhance their ethical awareness and decision-making.

19

Chapter 14: Utilizing Technology in Communication

In today's digital age, technology has become an indispensable tool for communication. This chapter explores how technology can enhance public speaking and leadership. From virtual presentations and webinars to social media and video conferencing, technology offers numerous platforms to reach and engage audiences. By leveraging these tools, leaders can expand their reach and connect with diverse groups in innovative ways.

One of the key advantages of technology is its ability to facilitate real-time interaction and feedback. Virtual platforms allow speakers to engage with audiences through polls, Q&A sessions, and interactive chats. This level of engagement can create a more dynamic and participatory experience, making the message more impactful. Additionally, technology enables the recording and sharing of presentations, allowing the content to reach a wider audience and have a lasting impact.

Another significant benefit of technology is its potential to enhance the accessibility of communication. Closed captioning, translation services, and screen reader compatibility are just a few examples of how technology can make content more inclusive. By considering the needs of diverse audiences and incorporating accessible features, leaders can ensure that their message is heard and understood by everyone.

However, it's important to recognize the challenges that come with technology. Technical issues, such as connectivity problems and software glitches, can disrupt communication and undermine the speaker's credibility. To mitigate these risks, it's essential to be well-prepared, conduct thorough rehearsals, and have backup plans in place. By mastering the use of technology and addressing potential challenges, leaders can harness its power to enhance their communication and leadership effectiveness.

20

Chapter 15: Building a Personal Brand

A strong personal brand is essential for establishing credibility and influence as a leader and public speaker. This chapter delves into the components of a personal brand and how to cultivate and maintain it. A personal brand encompasses one's values, expertise, and unique qualities that distinguish them from others. It is a reflection of how individuals present themselves to the world and how they are perceived by others.

Building a personal brand begins with self-reflection and understanding one's strengths, passions, and values. By identifying what sets them apart, individuals can articulate a clear and compelling personal brand statement. This statement should encapsulate their mission, vision, and the value they offer to their audience. It serves as a guiding compass for all communication and interactions.

Consistency is key to maintaining a strong personal brand. This involves aligning one's actions, messaging, and visual identity with their brand values and statement. Whether it's through social media posts, public appearances, or professional interactions, consistency builds trust and reinforces the brand's authenticity. It's also important to regularly review and adapt the personal brand to stay relevant and responsive to changing circumstances and audience expectations.

Finally, we explore strategies for amplifying and promoting a personal brand. Leveraging digital platforms, such as LinkedIn, Twitter, and personal

CHAPTER 15: BUILDING A PERSONAL BRAND

websites, can help individuals showcase their expertise and connect with a broader audience. Engaging in thought leadership activities, such as writing articles, speaking at events, and participating in industry forums, can further enhance their visibility and influence. By consistently delivering value and building meaningful connections, individuals can establish a strong and influential personal brand.

21

Chapter 16: The Future of Public Speaking and Leadership

The landscape of public speaking and leadership is continually evolving, shaped by technological advancements, social changes, and global trends. This chapter explores the future of these fields and the skills that will be essential for success. As technology continues to advance, new platforms and tools will emerge, offering innovative ways to communicate and engage with audiences. Virtual reality, augmented reality, and artificial intelligence are just a few examples of technologies that have the potential to revolutionize public speaking and leadership.

In addition to technological advancements, social and cultural changes will influence the way leaders communicate. The increasing emphasis on diversity, equity, and inclusion will require leaders to be more culturally competent and sensitive to the needs of diverse audiences. This involves understanding and addressing different perspectives, experiences, and expectations. Leaders who can navigate these complexities with empathy and respect will be better positioned to build trust and inspire action.

Another key trend is the growing importance of sustainability and social responsibility. As global challenges such as climate change, inequality, and health crises become more pressing, leaders will be expected to address these issues and advocate for positive change. Effective communication will be essential for raising awareness, mobilizing support, and driving collective action. Leaders who can articulate a clear vision for a sustainable and equitable future will be able to inspire and lead with impact.

Finally, the future of public speaking and leadership will be characterized by a greater focus on personal development and lifelong learning. The rapidly changing landscape will require leaders to continuously update their skills and knowledge. This involves staying informed about emerging trends, seeking feedback, and embracing new opportunities for growth. By committing to ongoing personal and professional development, leaders can remain agile and effective in an ever-changing world.

22

Chapter 17: Putting It All Together: Actionable Steps

In this final chapter, we bring together the key insights and strategies discussed throughout the book and provide actionable steps for applying them in practice. Effective communication and leadership require a holistic approach that integrates various skills and principles. By following these steps, individuals can enhance their public speaking and leadership capabilities and achieve their goals.

First, prioritize self-awareness and self-improvement. Understanding one's strengths, weaknesses, and areas for growth is the foundation for effective communication and leadership. Regularly seek feedback, reflect on experiences, and set specific goals for development. Embrace a growth mindset and view challenges as opportunities for learning and improvement.

Second, invest in preparation and practice. Whether it's for a speech, presentation, or difficult conversation, thorough preparation is essential. Create detailed outlines, rehearse regularly, and seek feedback from trusted peers. Practice active listening and empathy to understand and connect with the audience. By being well-prepared, individuals can build confidence and deliver impactful messages.

Third, leverage technology and digital platforms to enhance communication. Stay informed about emerging tools and trends, and experiment with

CHAPTER 17: PUTTING IT ALL TOGETHER: ACTIONABLE STEPS

different platforms to find what works best. Ensure that content is accessible and inclusive, considering the needs of diverse audiences. Be mindful of potential challenges and have backup plans in place to address technical issues.

Finally, cultivate a strong personal brand and lead with integrity. Articulate a clear and compelling personal brand statement that reflects one's values and expertise. Consistently align actions and messaging with the brand, and regularly review and adapt it to stay relevant. Lead by example, demonstrating authenticity, professionalism, and ethical behavior. By building trust and credibility, leaders can inspire bold actions and drive positive change.

Book Description: "Words in Motion: The Intersection of Public Speaking, Leadership, and Bold Action"

"Words in Motion: The Intersection of Public Speaking, Leadership, and Bold Action" is a comprehensive guide that explores the powerful synergy between eloquent communication, effective leadership, and decisive action. This book is an essential read for anyone looking to harness the power of words to inspire, persuade, and drive meaningful change in their personal and professional lives.

The book delves into the historical evolution of public speaking, tracing its roots from ancient times to the modern era. It highlights the influential figures and technological advancements that have shaped the art of oration and examines the future of communication in an increasingly digital world. Readers will gain insights into the timeless principles of rhetoric and how to adapt them to contemporary platforms.

At its core, "Words in Motion" emphasizes the importance of emotional intelligence, active listening, and ethical considerations in leadership. Through compelling stories, practical strategies, and real-life case studies, the book offers readers actionable steps to overcome public speaking anxiety, craft compelling narratives, and navigate difficult conversations with confidence and grace.

Ultimately, this book is a call to action for leaders to embrace their role as communicators and catalysts for change. By balancing authenticity with professionalism, leveraging technology, and building a strong personal brand, readers will learn how to inspire bold actions and lead with integrity. "Words in Motion" is a valuable resource for anyone seeking to make a lasting impact through the power of their words.

www.ingramcontent.com/pod-product-compliance
Lightning Source LLC
LaVergne TN
LVHW020457080526
838202LV00057B/6005